HE COMES

EFREM WHITEHURST

ISBN 979-8-89243-668-7 (hardcover)
ISBN 979-8-89243-669-4 (digital)

Christian Faith Publishing
832 Park Avenue
Meadville, PA 16335
www.christianfaithpublishing.com

Printed in the United States of America

CHAPTER 1

This story starts in the year 3030. Things seemed peaceful. There were no more engine-powered vehicles, diesel engines, factories, or anything that polluted or anything that caused the ozone layer to become thinner than what it had already become. The air seemed clearer—or was it?

On May 24, 3030, a child was born five in the morning, to be exact. This wasn't any ordinary child because of the events that happen to his biological mother. Nine months earlier, Ms. Norma Marie White became pregnant; you see, Norma was a quiet, sweet, loving daughter, who did very well in school, always honored her mother and father, and also participated in church activities.

Whatever went on in church, Norma was there. She loved God and Jesus dearly, and it showed in her talk, her walk; in other words, she walked the walk and talked the talk of God's words from the Bible. From the time she knew how to read, the first book she read was the Bible, and there were no other books that could top it.

On September 1, 3029, a strange thing happen to Norma. She went to bed at her usual time, 9:00 p.m., and kissed her mother and father good night. She went to her room, knelt down beside her bed, and said her prayers. "Lord God, bless my mother and my father, keep our house blessed with your loving goodness and mercy, and God bless me with someone who will love me and have no sin within him. In Jesus's name I pray. Amen."

You see, Norma never prayed about any other person in her life, except for her mother and father, but that night, God heard her so God's voice was all around her. In her mind, she thought it was just a dream until God showed his presence through his holy light. The warmth, the goodness she felt in this light, she knew it was only God. God told her, "There shall never be any other God like me. Through man, I shall make myself in you through child."

Norma couldn't believe what she was hearing, but she knew it was true. God said to her, "Your prayers I answered because blessed be the only one that has no sin within. For the last five years, there has been great turmoil in the world. All my children on earth have been fooled by their sinful activities." God then said unto her, "Behold, you are with child, and that child will be me. Thy mother and thy father will understand. I will go to them as I came to you through my holy light. Fear not as I grow in you, all things will be shown unto you. So shall it be, let it be done."

The first month of Norma's pregnancy was truly a learning experience for her. God told her things that she had no idea was going on. One day, when Norma and her mother, Marie Lynn White, were expected at Dr. Battle's office for Norma's first check up to see how herself and the fetus inside her were doing. Norma felt a great pain in heart. She didn't realize, at the time, what was going on, so she told her mother with tears in her eyes, "MOTHER! What's going to happen to me? My heart hurts so much!"

At that moment, a voice in her mind said to her, *Fear not, my child, what you feel in your heart is how hurt I am to the things that go on in the world today. Believe in what I say. I will not put on you a burden which thy heart cannot stand.*

When Norma heard God's words, calmness came to her heart. By this time, Norma and her mother arrived at the doctor's office by HTW. They checked in and waited to be called. With concern on her face, Norma's mother said to Norma, "Our family is truly blessed, baby. I knew in my heart you were special, Norma."

"Thank you, Mother," Norma replied.

But something seemed uneasy to Norma, and with that uneasiness Norma was feeling, she started looking at the women who were across from her.

Norma noticed the woman was in pain. Norma turned to her mother and said, "I must comfort her, Mother." Norma kissed her mother on the cheek and proceeded to go to the woman across from her.

The woman across from Norma was quietly moaning to herself, "God, please don't let anything happen to my baby."

Norma reached out her hand and said to the woman with a gentle voice, "Hello, excuse me, please, but I couldn't help but notice that you are in some kind of pain."

The woman looked at Norma and said, "Yes, I am, and the doctor is taking so long. Please excuse me. My name is Sarah."

"Nice to meet you, Sarah," Norma replied. "My name is Norma."

Norma felt a warm sense of comfort within her as if she knew everything that was going on inside. The woman's baby would be all right. Then, at that moment, she heard the voice say, *Give her your hand that I may heal the baby inside her.*

Norma knew who that was. It was God growing inside her, using her body to heal. Without hesitation, Norma reached out her hand to Sarah and said to her, "Take my hand, Sarah, let us pray."

Norma held Sarah's hand with one hand and placed the other hand on Sarah's belly and said, "God, we don't know what may lay ahead of us today, but with your power, strength, and wisdom, we know today is good. Watch over us, Lord, and give us the strength to carry on. In Jesus's name we pray. Amen."

A warm sensation came over the entire body of Sarah. Sarah then looked up at Norma and said to her, "O my God, Norma, the pain is gone. You are truly blessed with God's holy anointed hands."

Norma replied, "Thank you, Sarah. God has his hands on all the little children, even the unborn babies."

The intercom then loudly said, "Sarah Smith to room 106, please. Room 106. Sarah Smith."

Sarah thanked Norma again and went to room 106. "God bless you, Norma," said Sarah as she walked down the hall.

"God bless you, too, Norma." Norma never saw Sarah again after that day.

Norma went back to her mother and said, "Mother, did you see what happened?"

"Yes, I did," Norma's mother replied with tears in her eyes. "Yes, I did, baby." Norma's mother kissed Norma on her forehead and laid Norma's head on her shoulders. "Rest now, Norma. God has a lot in store for you. Rest, my precious one."

Twenty minutes had passed when, finally, Norma's name was called over the intercom. The doctor's visit went well. Everything was fine. On their way back home, Norma would repeatedly see visions in her mind.

At first, Norma couldn't understand the visions. Day after day, her visions became a burden on her. Her visions were of senseless deaths, of rape, explosions, bigotry, false prophets, and of the needed. Little did Norma know God was showing her his dislikes in the world today. So for eight months, God prepared Norma for his coming. On occasions, when Norma was out alone or with her family, sometimes, even with the few friends she had, God would use her physical body to bless those who were worthy of God's blessings.

On one particular day, Norma was out with one of her girl-friends, and, all of a sudden, Norma wanted her friend Susan and herself to get off the HTW (Human Transport Walkway). "Stop, let's get off! Susan, please, let us get off!" Norma said with a loud and nervous tone to her voice.

Without knowing why she had to get off, Susan grabbed Norma's hand and got off the HTW. "What's wrong, Norma?" Susan asked.

Norma, still nervous, replied, "I need to go into this building."

The building Norma was talking about was this old condemned church. God wanted Norma to feel the sorrow and hurt he was feeling because in this church, one man tried to make a difference. This man was so anointed with God's Holy Spirit. God and Jesus were very pleased with his ministries. This man of the cloth spoke the truth of the coming of the God. People thought he was crazy. One night at his church, his sermon was called "He's Coming," and the congregation belittled him and told him not to preach of false prophecies because his sermon was on the coming of God, not the coming of Jesus Christ as it was foretold in the Bible.

Little did his congregation know God gave him the foresight of his coming because of the disappointments with the world. God only wanted his Bible to show his love for the world, how to be better Christians, and show the world when Judgment Day comes, we will be with him as long as we followed his words. God also showed the pastor the things that disappointed him the most. "Why are my ministries using my Bible for financial gain, twisting my words in the Bible to kill my children because of wars that some call holy wars? Molestation in the church and bigotry. God loved this man of the cloth. His name was Pastor Redmond. God loved him and others like him because he not only spoke the truth of the things that are in the Bible but he also taught people how to understand what was to come. It wasn't about money or power. It was about *God*, his love for him, and his undeniable faithfulness to him. That's why God chose Pastor Redmond.

Norma saw what Pastor Redmond went through back when his church was open to all people. Susan grabbed Norma's hand and held it until she came from out of her trancelike state, and she did. "Susan!" Norma said with a high pitch in her voice, "God revealed to me the pastor of this church. He tried to tell the world of God's coming, and they thought he was crazy."

Norma and Susan were coming down the steps of the church when two men and three teenagers approached them and said, "What are you two girls doing in this old, abandoned building? Are you trying to get high or are you two trying to get your freak on? If so, can you two handle all of us?"

Norma looked at the one she believed to be the leader of the bunch and said to him, "No, it's not what you think. I had to come into this church. God told me to."

When Norma said that, the two men and three teenagers started to laugh at them. One man said, "God, right. I'll show you my god."

The man grabbed Norma by her hand with one hand and was trying to unzip his zipper with the other hand. At that moment, Norma's mouth open a very, very bright light appeared and a voice said, "Behold" for you have seen the light of God, go my son and sin

5

no more for I have delivered you from the darkness into the light, you and your friends go now and sin no more.

The two men and three teenagers dropped to their knees and said, "Please forgive us. God has shown us the light through you, and we will sin no more."

Susan couldn't believe her eyes. She saw God's light in her friend too a failed to her knees too. "Norma," Susan said, "I am not worthy to be your friend for I have sinned too."

"Susan," Norma said, "I forgave you a long time ago, and so has God."

After the men left, Norma was about to step down on the last step, when a very sharp pain went through her, and with that, God said, "It is time, my child, time for my coming."

CHAPTER 2

THE COMING

Susan knew she had to get Norma on the HTW as soon as possible. The pain Norma was having been great, but she knew she had to hold on. Norma still having visions of Pastor Redmond vision the pastor in the year 2007 until his death. God showed Norma Pastor Redmond and others like him in his kingdom up in heaven, awaiting God's command to return to earth as his generals Holy Army of truth and glory.

God explained to Norma that the pains she was having are one of the burdens women have to have because of Eve's behavior in the garden of Eden. Eve didn't trust in God. She listened to the serpent, so the pain they must stand. Norma, holding her belly, said to Susan, "Susan, he's coming! My Lord and Savior is coming!" Norma then began to have flashbacks of Jesus's life and the price Jesus paid to save us from our sins.

Norma realized she was in the hospital, in the delivery room with her mother by her side. Susan and Norma's father were waiting in the waiting room. While in the waiting room, Norma's father, John Peter White, said to Susan, "Let us pray."

So the two held hands, and John started to pray, "God, my heavenly Father, I am weak, but you are strong. You and only you can make the turmoil in the world today end, and I know, with your coming, it will soon be done. When my time has ended, I hope I am worthy of your blessings. In Jesus's name I pray. Amen."

Susan looked at Mr. White and said to him, "Excuse me, Mr. White, but why didn't you pray for your daughter? I think it was very selfish of you to pray for yourself."

Mr. White looked at Susan and, with a smile on his face, said to her, "Susan, I've prayed for my daughter every day since she became impregnated with child, the Lord God himself, so I figured that God already has my daughter in good hands and is all right, so please let it be okay, just this once, for me to ask if I am worthy of God's love too. That's all I was doing, Susan."

Susan looked at Mr. White and smiled and said, "I apologize, Mr. White. How selfish of me to think that you weren't thinking of Norma. Please accept my apology."

Mr. White gave Susan a hug and kisses on her forehead and said, "Susan, you don't have to apologize to me. You have always been a very good friend to Norma, and I always appreciated that."

Susan looked up at Mr. White and smiled and laid her head on his chest and closed her eyes and said, "Thank you."

After that, they both sat down and waited until someone came out the delivery room to give them some good news.

Today is May 24, 3030, 4:50 a.m., and all I can think about is the day and time. That's what Norma was thinking about in her mind, but that's what God wanted her to remember—the time and date. Norma looked up at her mother and said, "Mother, thank you for being here with me. I think Susan wouldn't have been in any shape to handle this."

They both laughed out loud at each other, and Norma was holding her belly, and right at that moment, Norma yelled out, "OH GOD, MOTHER! HE'S COMING! OH MY GOD!"

Mother said," "NURSE, GET THE DOCTOR! HURRY!"

The nurse, without hesitation, called the doctor. "Dr. Battle to delivery room 1, please! Dr. Battle to delivery room 1."

It was like the doctor had already known. He was standing at the wash area, getting prepared. Then the time and date flashed in Norma's mind: May 24, 3030, 5:00 a.m. and, sure enough, *plop!* The baby was in the doctor's hands. The doctor couldn't believe how easy it was for Norma. He said to Norma, "The only thing you said was,

'Oh God, Mother, he's coming,' and wham! There he is. When I pulled him out, I could have sworn the baby looked at me and said, 'Thank you. Be blessed,' but I was wrong, three deliveries in one day. Boy, I believe the crying of the baby sounded like he was talking to me."

The doctor then cut the lifeline of mother and child that had been used by God to fill the baby's human flesh with God's essence and Spirit. Doctor Battle had the baby cleaned and placed in Norma's arms. The baby looked up at Norma, and Norma could read the baby's mind. *It has been done, so now let us begin this holy quest together to free my children from Satan's grips*, the baby said to Norma.

Norma then looked at her mother and said, "I will call him Jeh, short for Jehovah."

The baby smiled. Norma knew God was pleased.

"Jehovah Christian White."

Norma's mother said, "That's beautiful, honey."

After a few minutes, two nurses came and got the baby to be cleaned and got Norma cleaned up and to her room too. Thirty minutes had passed when, finally, Norma was reunited with her baby and family in her private room. There was a peaceful, joyous-like feeling about the room. Baby Jeh was wide awake, noticing everything and even noticing his human body.

Mr. and Mrs. White and Susan were standing around Norma's bed, and Mr. White said, "Let us pray" when, all of a sudden, Dr. Battle came rushing into the room.

"Excuse me, please, but I have some amazing news! I just got back your baby's test, along with his blood work, and I couldn't believe my own eyes or what I heard. You have the healthiest baby in the world and, not only that, his blood, Lord have mercy, and your baby's blood was being taken to be stored in the lab when the intern stumbled, and the vial, which contained the blood, hit the floor and broke. The blood went everywhere.

"The blood got on Mrs. Paul's forehead, and without reason, Mrs. Paul lifted her head up, opened her eyes, and said, 'Thank you, God, for I was once in darkness, but now I'm free, for it was your blood that delivered me! Thank you, Lord, thank you.' Norma, Mr.

and Mrs. White," the doctor said with excitement in his voice, "I wouldn't have believed it if it wasn't for Mrs. Paul. You see, Mrs. Paul has been blind for two years and had a stroke last year that left her unable to talk or walk. That's why I know your baby is blessed with God's love and mercy.

"We must not tell a soul because there are a lot of people in this day and time who don't believe in God or Jesus, like we do."

Mr. White was about to say something when the doctor said, "Don't worry about the intern. He's a Christian, too, just like us. He won't say a word."

So Mr. White told the doctor the events that happened to his daughter and who the baby is. Dr. Battle fell to his knees, beside the bed, and looked at Norma and the baby with tears in his eyes and said, "Norma, I don't know if your baby can understand me, but all my adult life, I've been helping people, some bad and some good. Just this once, I would like to help God as I should and spread his Word, no matter where I'm at."

Norma touched the doctor on the top of his head and said, "God heard you, and he's glad you love him and his Son. Be blessed, and don't stop spreading his Word because he has something in store for you."

The doctor burst out in tears and said, "Thank you, Lord. I will spread your Word, Lord, I will." Dr. Battle then told the family and Susan he was going to release Norma and Jeh today because he was afraid that someone in the hospital might find out about the baby and try to contact the Antichrist.

The time was 11:05 a.m., and Norma was now released from the hospital. On the way home, Norma's father stopped to get their HTH (Human Transport Hover) energized at the One Stop Convenience Store, just two miles from his house. As Mr. White pulled up to the energizer pump, Jeh began to cry. Right next to them was an old man in a replica of an old, beat up, Ford pickup truck mounted on his HTH with a piece of cardboard on the passenger side of the back window. It read "God hides, the devil smiles, but God's not far. Just a couple of miles."

Jeh then became quiet as he looked in his mother's eyes. Norma could see the piece of cardboard. Norma said, "Dad, the old man on the other side of the pump, read what's on the piece of cardboard on the back window."

Mr. White pressed firmly on the handle so he could lock the energizer line into the HTH to keep the nuclear energy flowing in the compact nuclear generator while he read what was on the piece of cardboard. Mr. White couldn't believe his eyes. *How could this old man know?* he thought to himself, but Mr. White had to find out for himself if this old man knew God was nearer than he thought. Mr. White approached the old man and said, "Excuse me, but I was noticing the piece of cardboard on your window, and I couldn't help but wonder, why did you write that? Of all things to write, why that?"

The old man replied, "Hello, my name is Lucas. What's yours?"

Mr. White replied, "John."

The old man said, "That's a good name, an honest and true name, and the piece of cardboard on my window means he is coming soon, so God has to hide while the devil smiles from all the stuff he's causing on earth, but God's day will come, and it will be just a couple of miles from here. That's what God tells me in my dreams and thoughts."

Mr. White looked at the old man and said, "He's nearer to coming than you think."

The old man looked over into Mr. White's car and said, "That's your family?"

"Yes," Mr. White replied.

So the old man walked over to the front window to introduce himself to Mrs. White first, "Hello there, young lady. My name is Lucas, Lucas Angel."

Mrs. White answered back, "I'm Mary, and this is my daughter, Norma, and her newborn baby Jeh, short for Jehovah."

The old man looked in the back seat, and right at that moment, everything around them froze in time, except for them. Jeh opened his mouth, and the light of God appeared. The old man, who was once slumped over, straightened up, and the prettiest light you could have ever imagined appeared around him. He was in white, the clothes he had on disappeared, and wings appeared. The old man was no longer old. Lucas said, "God, I have waited for thee. You have arrived and set me free, so now I will protect thee and the White family."

The old replica of a truck that was once at the other energizer pump had disappeared, along with Lucas. Mr. White looked at his wife and smiled. "Honey, God had his angel here all the time protecting us. Jeh knew this all along."

Just as everything froze, everything went back to normal, so Mr. White thought. He proceeded home with his family in his HTH. Back at the White's house, Norma and Jeh were up in her room, and Jeh was putting visions in Norma's mind. God knew when he changed Lucas back into an angel, his powers would be recognized by evil, but he had to transform not only Lucas back into an angel but also thousands of others who had been here on earth since the year 2000 in human form.

God knew he had to work quickly because the Antichrist was coming to try to stop Jesus from coming back. The Antichrist and Satan had no idea that God himself was already here. God showed Norma the reason of his coming. He showed Norma, back in the Roman era, when Romans gathered at the colosseum to see his children fight and battle to the death for sport and entertainment, and his animals starved, just to battle his children also to their deaths. He told her how Satan fooled his children into thinking that this was a form of entertainment. He showed her how he cleansed the world of this evil, when he flooded the earth and let Noah and his family and the animals start the world anew, but Satan got his grips on mankind again.

"Satan started fooling my children into believing that coliseums, stadiums, and fighting rings were good for entertainment—the more violent the sport, the more people would watch, and the more money you will make. Satan has caused great turmoil and confusion in men by also fooling them into believing that there is profit in prostituting of women and children, and using my plants that I put of the earth to help the sick to use as a mind-altering drug for profit.

"I say unto thee money is the root of all evil. I didn't mean for my children to prosper like this. All your riches shall await you in the kingdom of heaven. I say unto thee, give to the needed. Everyone on earth should be equal in wealth, not poor." God also showed Norma how Satan did the same to his ministers, bishops, evangelists, and prophets who used the words of the Bible to gain the trust of his or her congregation for greed, lust, bigotry, molestation, backstabbing of one's own brother or sister, and twisted his ministers' minds to get them to take from his children to gain power and wealth.

"Satan has my ministries in damnation of doom! My ministers have bodyguards to protect them. Why has thy lost faith in me? I told my children, 'Who that believe in me shall have everlasting life, I will be their protector, but yet they are afraid of their own people because of greed.'

"Some have used my Bible to twist my words to go to another country to kill my children and even go back home to kill their own if you don't believe in their cause. I had to come and rid my world of the forces of this kind of evil.

"Norma, my child and my human mother by flesh, a lot of my children will perish if they don't repent, cast out the demons they hold, show thy love and faithfulness for me. If not, thy will not fight this upcoming holy war with me, GOD ALMIGHTY."

When God was finished, Norma told her father to spread the word of God's coming, and he did. Mr. White gathered all who believed, along with his wife, Dr. Battle, and Susan. God summoned Pastor Redmond, his angels, and all others who awaited God's commands in his kingdom in heaven to come and stand by him. Jesus would come later to fight. God knew the Antichrist and the forces of evil were close at hand, but he didn't want death and destruction near the home of his chosen one. "The land on which this house stands shall be holy. No evil shall penetrate its walls."

After God told Norma all of this, they rested. Baby Jeh and his mother slept with a smile on their faces, knowing no evil shall come to their house. Overseas, a strange thing was happening. There were massive earthquakes and volcanic activities where there were no reported earthquakes or volcanos at all. This was because Satan knew of the coming, but he was disappointed in his followers. Not even his demons or his so-called Antichrist could locate the gathering of God's army. That's why there were unexpected earthquakes and volcanos because of Satan's anger. Satan summoned his Antichrist to appear before him, and he did. The man was ruler of all nations. There were no more separations of countries or kings, queens, dictators, or presidents. *No*, it was only one ruler, and it was him, the Antichrist.

His name was Damian Lusafor. He was a quiet, soft-spoken man with power, evil power, and some believed in this man. Some thought of him as the savior of mankind, but those who were true to God's words saw right through him. They knew he had to be stopped somehow, so the people of the true word of Christians remained in hiding until the day of the gathering. Satan said unto Damian, "You call yourself the Antichrist. Some call you the savior of mankind. The true Christians of Christ know exactly who you are but, why, for the life of me, can't you find a bunch of holy worshippers?

"WHY! Are is it you are not worthy of me. I'm the one who granted you with the power to control all things living of this earth, to alter the thoughts of others to only see the goodness in you, not the evilness inside you, but you just can't seem to control all, can you? Is the love of God that strong in others? Or is it you're not trying hard enough to get through to these Christians? I suggest you follow the Word of God, just as I did once, and then when you have their trust in you, use your power to turn them against God and his so-called begotten Son, and then and only then you'll have total control of God's Christians.

"Now leave me. I have a lot of planning to do. BE GONE!"

Satan sent Damian back, and he started having his followers try to find where the Christians were having their meeting so he could start his followers and himself go to such meetings to gain their trust. All over the world, where there were broadcasting stations, Damian was telling of his love for God and how the true Christians of Christ would once again save us all with God's undeniable love and glory. Damian just didn't know how true this was.

Back at the White's home, there was great celebration because God, who was once a baby in human flesh, has transformed himself into a man.

"Norma," God said to her, "it is time now of the gathering, and I have to leave my infant form and become a man so I can communicate with you and others by word of mouth."

Norma told her family and the other followers of God's transformation into a man, and they rejoiced and prayed unto him. Norma's father got on his knees in front of God's manlike body and said a prayer unto him, "We now can see and hear you speak by word of mouth, my Lord. Thank you for this blessed day, and we will continue to follow you through trying times. No matter what happens, we will always love and follow thee. In Jesus's name we pray. Amen."

Jeh looked down at Mr. White and said, "Stand, please, my earthly grandfather. With tears in my eyes, I praise and honor thee. You and Grandmother planted the seed, and I gave it life. This life I speak of is Norma, and with her kindness and goodness, I became one in she, so now I'm truly blessed to have an earthly family."

CHAPTER 3

THE GATHERING

All of the followers of God and Christ where now congregating in the field. God called this field the Great Field of Glory because once in this great field stood a holy cross. This cross was a gateway to God's kingdom. Every great man or woman who loved God came through its corridor of heavenly light, such as all the people who tried to help stop bigotry, slavery, and wars. But there were those who hated the cross and what it stood for, so they burned it down and would kill anyone who would try to build another in its place, but little did they know God still granted this field holy in his name. Christians knew of this, but not evil. Here was the Antichrist's chance. The demons of hell could sense an overwhelming sense of goodness close to them because the great number of God's followers were in this field. The demons picked up on all this goodness very easily. So now it was a chance of a lifetime to make Satan proud of him, now that he knew he could make Satan happy by finding the whereabouts of the gathering.

Damian got together some of his best night stalkers. These humanlike demons were like no other demon because of their ability to hide in the shadows. They could hide in the smallest shadow during the day, and by night, they were totally invisible, unless they came into the light. Once they came in contact with light during the night, they froze in time for about twenty seconds. This was enough time to destroy these evil creatures with anointed holy water or oil, that's why these demons chose only to do their devilish work at night. Damian called these creatures Drackens. The Drackens located the field of the gathering. They did so by being around those who hated the Christians because they thought the Christians were the cause of the destruction that was going on. They believed that all the earthquakes and volcanic activities that were happening was God's anger.

They also believed that all who believed in the words of the Bible use the Bible for profit and power over others; that's why these people turned their backs on the gathering and started backstabbing and putting the word of the Bible down so that gave the Drackens the opportunity to locate the gathering during the day. By their disbeliefs, the Drackens were able to hide in the disbelievers. One simply shadow casted below the neck or behind the ear was all it took to get the Drackens the information they needed for their Lord Damian.

With this information, the Darckens hurried back to Damian. Damian summoned Satan. "My true and worthy ruler of the heavens above, I summon you to appear before me. I am your humble servant and will do your bidding."

At that moment, the room became dark, the floor opened, and the fires of hell came out, and then Satan appeared. "Why are you demanding my presence, Damian? I hope there is news of the gathering."

"Yes, my lord Satan, I have very good news of this gathering. The Drackens located them, and now we can destroy them all."

"That is good news, my son. You will be well rewarded for this, you and your Drackens. Now I must go back to my kingdom in hell for now, but heaven will be mine when I destroy the Christians and Jesus. That will cause God to be angered by this and lose his power of goodness and mercy. That's when he'll be on the dark side, my domain. HA-HA-HA! Heaven awaits its true God, SATAN! GOD WILL BE AT MY KNEES, ASKING FOR FORGIVENESS!" After Satan said that, he disappeared back into the pits of hell.

Damian summoned all who followed Satan's rule to form their own gathering back in the deserted lands of the hottest climate, the desert, to await the commands of Satan himself. Damian was so caught up with his victory over Jesus and the Christians he forgot one thing—the Drackens only picked up on the gathering of the Christians and Jesus because of the hate the disbelievers had for the Christians. Little did they know that God Almighty himself would command his holy army, not Jesus. Back in hell, Satan was planning his greatest and most diabolical war plan to defeat the holy ones. Satan relayed his plans to his greatest warriors. The leader of the warriors was Mon'zar.

Mon'zar was also Satan's best soul collector. He collected billions of once humble and honest people's souls on earth for Satan's pleasure. Mon'zar did this by trickery or by catching people when they lost their faith in God or fooling them into thinking he was sent by God to deliver them from evil, which this also fall into trickery too.

Satan told Mon'zar, "Mon'zar, on the day of the gathering, get your men and women that have already sold their soul to me to continue their friendship with the Christians and have the Christians believe they are on their side to triumph over me. Once you gain their trust, they will lead you to the gathering. Spread out, have two of your men behind Jesus, and have your Drackens in the shadows of the rest of the leaders and the Christian army."

CHAPTER 4

SATAN'S CHANCE

"Then, when all is ready, I will appear in front of Jesus and his leaders, and that's when the two behind Jesus take him captive. This will be my chance of victory because God doesn't want his Son to perish in my hands, so I will make God himself come down from the heavens above to spare his Son's life. As soon as God appears, tell the Drackens to attack. Start taking the Christians into their own shadows and kill them. Once God hears the suffering and murder of his children and his Son, his goodness and mercy will be his downfall, and that's when God and his Son dies."

Now Satan had his plans in order, and he sent his army out to expedite his plans of victory over goodness. Little did Norma or the other Christians know that all around them were the devil's warriors and followers. Norma was sensing something close to her, but she couldn't see or hear anything. Norma went to Jeh and explained to him what kind of feelings she was having. Jeh stopped and looked straight into Norma's eyes and said to her in his human form, "Fear not, Mother, for it will come to pass that you will be casted down into darkness. Evil will try to take your life as well as our family and Christian friends."

Norma couldn't understand why Jeh would tell her this—why would God let his children die?—but she didn't question Jeh. She left it in God's hands as she was taught to do. Jeh commanded the Christians to meet at the gathering. Jeh then called on his angels and the rest of his followers in heaven to come down to earth to join the others at the gathering. Once all was ready, Jeh would stand before his army with his leaders at his side.

The moment had arrived. Jeh said, "Send our deliverer down from heaven so thy will be done over evil."

This was the moment Satan was waiting for. He told his army, with his mind, to get ready, and they did. The Drackens were in the Christians' shadows, the devil's followers were also in the gathering, and the two warriors were behind Jeh, awaiting for Jesus to appear.

Jeh looked up into the heavens, and then he closed his eyes and said, "BEHOLD, for he is coming, and with him there shall be everlasting light."

Right at that moment, a light appeared right in front of Jeh. A form was inside the light. The Christians were holding their heads down, saying, "We praise thee, sweet Jesus. Lead us into battle, for thou art with us, and no weapons or evil shall prosper."

Just as the light was about to disappear, Satan appeared and commanded his army to attack. As soon as the followers and warriors of Satan did so, Jeh opened his mouth, but no words came out. The heavenly Spirit and light of God came out. God took hold of Satan, then his holy light was all around his true Christian followers and leaders. God said to Satan, "Behold, Satan, for I am God. There will be no other God but me. You have deceived my children and tried to turn them against me. Behold what my goodness and mercy bring."

Satan looked out into the gathering, and his army of warriors was on their knees, in front of their mothers, fathers, brothers, and sisters, asking God for forgiveness.

"For you, Satan, have kept them in darkness, not knowing the true glory of my light. For those in your army that have found the light shall dwell in my house forever, and those who didn't shall perish with you and the rest of your followers forever. There will be no more darkness and sorrow on earth forevermore. So it shall be. Let it be done."

With God's mighty powers, Satan and the disbelievers of Christ were no more. The earth was once again pure. God's angels gathered together the devil's warriors who changed from the darkness and came into the light and followed God and the rest of the followers back to heaven.

Norma looked up, and God said to her, "Norma, look down at your feet for thou has been truly a blessing to me. Your prayer I did answer for you to find someone to love you and is without sin. Remember, Norma, the time is 5:00 a.m., May 24, 3030. I give you your human baby, Jeh, who is blessed with my holy light. Love him and cherish him. Be blessed, my child."

Norma, with tears in her eyes, said, "Thank you, God. I will always love my baby and cherish you too. Thank you."

Everyone gathered around Norma, and the baby said, "Thank you. He came, God Almighty came and helped us. Thank you."

Amen.

ABOUT THE AUTHOR

I was born and raised in Portsmouth, Virginia, and now I live in Durham, North Carolina. I am a strong believer in God, but I became lost in the world of drugs and alcohol. When I finally rebuked the life I was living without my Lord and Savior, Jesus Christ, in it, I gave my life back to God. Now all things are possible. God's words delivered me from all my addictions. God restored my soul. Now my life is good and truly blessed. My marriage is beautiful, and my job is awesome all because I put God first in all I do.

Printed in the USA
CPSIA information can be obtained
at www.ICGtesting.com
LVHW091151200624
783484LV00010B/419/J